YOUR KNOWLEDGE HAS VALUE

Bibliographic information published by the German National Library:

The German National Library lists this publication in the National Bibliography; detailed bibliographic data are available on the Internet at http://dnb.dnb.de .

Imprint:

Copyright © 2012 GRIN Verlag, Open Publishing GmbH
Print and binding: Books on Demand GmbH, Norderstedt Germany
ISBN: 9783668381360

This book at GRIN:

http://www.grin.com/en/e-book/351392/technology-and-innovation-how-does-the-strategic-planning-process-impact

Fotini Mastroianni

Technology and innovation. How does the strategic planning process impact the management of technology and innovation and what consideration is given to the impact of disruptive technologies in particular?

GRIN Publishing

GRIN - Your knowledge has value

Since its foundation in 1998, GRIN has specialized in publishing academic texts by students, college teachers and other academics as e-book and printed book. The website www.grin.com is an ideal platform for presenting term papers, final papers, scientific essays, dissertations and specialist books.

Visit us on the internet:

http://www.grin.com/

http://www.facebook.com/grincom

http://www.twitter.com/grin_com

How does the strategic planning process impact the management of technology and innovation and what considerations are given to the impact of disruptive technologies in particular?

Use your library or your favorite Internet search engine and find two examples of a successful innovation and one that was not so successful. (Finding failures is difficult.) Critically analyse what were the reasons given for success? For failure? Which of these reasons relate to poor planning? What does this tell you about the keys to success in innovation?

Table of contents

Introduction

International experience shows constantly, through studies and practical applications, that fostering innovation relies more on strategic planning, research and search for specific data. The development of business strategy would have never been more challenging or more important than in today's competitive environment through which corporate strategies must transcend past limits.

The paper analyzes three case studies. All of them are innovative companies however technology was used as part of their innovation for Easy Jet and Korres, whereas in PARC it was its core business. In the case of the two successful innovators Korres S.A. and Easy Jet, technology dealt with the development of the company's R&D (Korres), it was used as a facilitator of processes which were the key factor for lowering production costs (Easy Jet) and finally in the case of PARC – Xerox technology was not focused on customer needs.

Corporate Strategy – Strategic Planning

Corporate Strategy is the result of strategic thinking, which is a design process that implements innovation, strategic planning and operational planning. Strategic thinking is a mindset that focuses on finding and exploiting unique opportunities to create attractive returns on invested capital and added value to shareholders. Innovation is a way to find unique opportunities; however, it should be part of a company's strategic thinking and culture (Pashmore, 1994). The companies that will be analyzed below, Korres and Easy Jet have this mindset and innovation is a basic part of their strategy whereas the other company PARC, although, it innovated, the lack of strategic thinking on customer focus led it to failure.

More and more managers now find that the experiences of the past are not always the best basis for developing future strategies but they need to innovate to keep ahead of competition (Chan & Mauborgne, 2000).

Strategic planning is a process of determining long-term goals and selecting implementation policies and is based on scientific analysis, international experience and participatory processes Innovation and technological innovation are a major strategic decision of a company, thus strategic planning is an integral part of the strategy implementation process (Bower & Christensen, 1995).

Business & Successful Innovation

There are several characteristics of successful innovators. As it happens with all successful businesses, they understand the importance of financial liquidity. Their major way of generating profits is not by setting high prices but at keeping low their production costs. They improve their internal processes aiming at improving manufacturing capabilities. A number of them decides to outsource certain activities. In case, they do not have technological capabilities, they may decide to form strategic alliances with companies that are technologically better (Stringer, 2000:81).

In case, product costs are high and product price cannot be decreased, successful innovators find other ways to reach their target group such as leasing the product.

According to Page (1993) successful innovators should do up-front homework i.e. they should not move from the creation of the idea to its implementation but they should prepare an appropriate plan of it. Successful innovators are customer centered and offer superior value to their customers. They plan carefully product launches and they have dedicated, well organized functional teams. They also have strong leaders and international orientation.

Strategic planning – Technology and disruptive technologies

In many cases, technological innovation exceeds market requirements. It is true that companies compete for technological advancement however, they miss the element of speed i.e. they over satisfy customers' needs thus leaving space for disruptive technologies to enter since lower price points exist. This is the point where Korres S.A. and Easy Jet entered. For example, other cosmetic companies were focused on the classic competition i.e. adding new products to their existing product lines that were using chemical substances. Even, the Body Shop that has a nature friendly profile, did not focus on specific herbs thus there was enough space for Korres S.A. to enter the particular market in Greece first and later worldwide.

According to Utterback (1996), unsuccessful firms defend excessively their technologies, which have reached high levels of design, when their business death is predictable.

Managers, unfortunately, can realize the value of disruptive technology only in retrospect. They can notice that disruptive technologies are usually developed by either new companies or by large ones that want to enter a new market segment. The best thing the managers can do is to watch carefully the new products launched. A disruptive technology requires a new management approach that has nothing to do with preconceived strategies but is involved with continuous learning and has adequate plans for learning. Tracking technological discontinuities is difficult; however, a company should always watch carefully its environment. Companies need to search not only for existing sources of competition but also for sources that are not conventional (Bower & Christensen, 1995).

According to Christensen (1997) managers should approach this disruptive business by having in mind that they do not know this new area therefore they will be able to recognize useful information and not invest massively in capital and time. In other words, a different way of thinking is required when a business wants to implement a radical innovation. Successful innovations quite often are not something particularly new in technology or science as it is seen with the examples of successful information mentioned below. What successful innovators are interested in is the search for segments that will be satisfied with the present performance levels. They are characterized by marketing orientation and satisfaction of market segments that were neglected by competition. They create teams of people that focus on new technologies and make improvements in accordance with customer feedback. If the company is too big to change its culture then a separate company can be created to perform these changes and produce innovative products at small volumes. As Stringer suggested (2000:72)" the attacking and defending ought to be done in separate organizations."

Utterback (1996) suggested a specific pattern of innovations. He noticed that discontinuous innovations in assembled products come from outside the specific sector whereas the discontinuous innovations in non assembled products may come either from inside or outside the sector. Regarding changes, he observed that discontinuous changes that concern processes in homogeneous products derive usually form established companies. It is understood that when discontinuities expand a market then newcomers will enter but when they do not broaden it then companies that already exist will get a better place.

It is also remarked that innovations that augment a company's core competencies usually come from inside the industry whereas the opposite happens when core competencies are destroyed. This is particularly in the case of Korres S.A. that will be analyzed below.

Successful innovations

Two companies of Greek businessmen, Korres S.A. and Easy Jet will be presented as examples of successful innovation.

KORRES S.A.

Korres SA is a Greek natural cosmetics company. The company initially produced one product but now produces more than five hundred different products, including specific categories. In Greece, Korres products are present in more than six thousand pharmacies whereas abroad they have a significant presence in branded chains of thirty countries and they also have twenty-seven stores in major cities worldwide (Koutra,2009). The company has invested in research and development for new formulations and new ingredients as well as in new technologies that help create new innovative products based on Greek nature. The composition of the company's products is based on four major groups of natural ingredients (Dimitriou, 2008): a) the Greek flora herbs b) herbs with medicinal properties, c) food ingredients, d) natural raw material. Thus, by using these natural ingredients innovative formulas are created, non-natural substances are avoided and replaced with natural oils and more compatible raw material. The company also cooperates with the University of Athens by participating in development projects of industrial research aiming at finding properties of the medicinal plants of the Greek flora. It also works with the Chios Gum Mastic Growers Association to develop products with mastic and it also works with the Saffron producers Cooperative of Kozani, for distributing exclusively Kozani organic saffron through pharmacies and exporting it overseas (Koutra, 2009).

Korres is really competitive and its marketing is very active this is why it has a leading position in the Greek cosmetics market and gains ground abroad

Korres is a successful innovator and this is due to two basic reasons: a strategy that focuses on innovation (Govindarajan, 2011) and the whole organization is fully aligned to this strategy (well organized functional teams, non authoritative corporate culture, motivated employees) and senior management i.e. Korres is personally involved (he is the head of the R&D department whereas his wife is the head of Marketing department, both of them are pharmacists). According to Govindarajan (2011) when the person who is responsible for the

5

investment and expenses is actively involved in the innovation process then more freedom is provided to the research team and thus big innovative ideas are created.

EASY JET

Easy Jet transformed the European aviation industry by making air travel affordable for everyone.

Easy Jet has low prices due to the non-issuance of tickets printed. A passenger just needs his/her passport and reservation code. Additionally, Easy Jet minimizes costs by not working with travel agencies. The abolition of cooperation with agents and the non issuance of tickets reduces the cost of the ticket price by 25%. Another significant cut made by Easy Jet for the reduction of the cost of air tickets concerns the meals offered during the flight (Smyroglou, 2010). Easy Jet passengers have the option to buy drinks or snacks from EasyKiosk (Easy Jet, 2012).

Furthermore, the company uses main destination airports throughout Europe, which have high fees. However, it uses the fleet effectively and saves money by keeping the processing time of ground operations at an average of 25 minutes. In addition, Easy Jet makes agreements with the airports for progressively decreasing fees (Easy Jet, 2012). By reducing the time spent on the ground Easy Jet can have extra flights on busy routes, thereby it maximizes the utilization of its aircraft.

The company manages to keep fares low, because it can exploit the best fuel use and the low maintenance cost due to the fact that its aircraft is new (it is the newest in the world) (Easy Jet, 2012).

There is no business class in Easy Jet planes and as a result more people are served and more tickets are issued. In addition, the seats are not numbered in the aircraft, so someone can sit wherever he wishes. Boarding in the aircraft is done in accordance with the order the passengers hand over their luggage and receive their boarding passes. So, especially in short flights, all these cuts allow a significant reduction in ticket price.

The non determination of allowed weight for hand luggage is also innovation. Thus, the passenger can take with him his hand luggage regardless of weight, as soon as s/he can carry it (Easy Jet, 2012). This way time is saved time upon arrival at the airport and fast travelers are facilitated.

Cheap air ticket is certainly not invented by the founder of Easy Jet, Stelios Chatziioannou. Simply, the gifted young entrepreneur followed the footsteps of the

U.S.airlines that introduced the spirit of liberalization in air transport (Athanasiou, 2008). This means that the Europeans now fly cheap. Nowadays, what is noticed is that Easy Jet actions are followed by other companies. Virgin Atlantic is attempting something similar, and even British Airways seems to move to this direction (Papanikolaou, 2010).

Easy Jet aims at making continuous improvements on its basic corporate philosophy i.e. offering cheap air travel.

According to Cooper and Kleinschmidt (1993) a successful innovator should be customer centered and offer unique benefits and superior value for the customer. Page (1993) adds that strong leadership, accountable work teams and international orientation are also needed for successful innovation. Easy Jet is customer oriented and its innovation lies more on improving its processes to offer superior value to its customers. It would not have been successful if this innovation process was not marked by the strong personality of Stelios Chatziioannou and the well organized and internationally oriented functional teams that focus on offering superior customer value.

Unsuccessful innovation – Xerox and PARC

In 1970, Xerox has created PARC which was its research center aiming at developing technology. PARC became a Xerox subsidiary in 2002 after having developed a number of revolutionary computer products such as the prototype of the modern PC etc (Xerox, 2012). Although, PARC was known for its technological excellence, Xerox did not manage to take advantage of this excellence. Researchers think (Waldrop, 2001) that this was due to the casual culture that was dominant at PARC and that allowed employees to pursue projects that they liked without paying any attention to the potential commercial value of the projects. A further failure reason was that PARC was far away from Xerox headquarters so there was bad communication and mismatch of goals between PARC employees and headquarters employees (Waldrop, 2001).

According to Kim and Mauborgne (2000) successful innovators focus on customers and more specifically on how the product meets the customers' needs and they are not solely oriented on developing technology as PARC did. Bad innovations do not look at how the customer buys, gets and uses the product, in other words their product development is not customer oriented.

Conclusion

As it is seen in the case studies above, technology is important but it is not the most important factor for successful innovation. Technology should be in accordance with market trends and consumer factors. Businesses should look for promising market segments. However, they should expect that at the beginning people resist to new ideas (Chan & Mauborgne, 2000:131).

The above companies, when they started were new, however now they are well established. They have managed to have their own product lines that bring them the cash required for the well being of the company, however, they need to take new initiatives and find the balance between established profitable products and new ones that are risky. Even, in the established products they need to improve them continuously (i.e. product improvement and process design improvement). Products should be monitored carefully.

There is a continuous struggle on the side of the companies i.e. they have to reduce costs to remain competitive. Production costs can be reduced by using better materials, human resources and energy, simplify processes and eliminate products and product lines that are not profitable. These actions can be characterized as defending the existing corporate position but companies should further develop their core skills and capabilities to remain competitive. Korres, for example, has a good research and development department specialized in the properties of Greek herbs, By taking advantage of this core skill, they decided to enter to the food ingredients sector by allying with the Mastic and Saffron cooperatives. This movement was part of its strategic planning process whereas the company decided to regenerate business by moving to new segments.

Korres and Easy Jet have managed to find the right strategy i.e. they focus on their core policy, however, Korres has also managed to diversify its product line whereas Easy Jet has managed to diversify by improving its internal processes. Both companies have focused on other activities rather than solely on their core skills since by focusing only on their own skills there may be a danger of being vulnerable to innovations that require different capacities. However, they managed both not to spread themselves too thin.

It is difficult for companies to manage the combination of the above but the ones that manage to do it become the winners.

Reference List

Athanasiou, S.2008. (in Greek), *Stelios Chatziioannou, an economic immigrant.* Accessed [16 March 2012]. Available from the World Wide Web: http://www.mediashipping.gr/?q=node/910

Bower, J.L. and Christensen, C.1995.Disruptive technologies: Catching the wave, *Harvard Business Review*, January-February.

Chan, K. and Mauborgne, R. 2000.Knowing a winning business idea when you see one, *Harvard Business Review*, September-October 2000,pp.129-138.

Christensen, C. 1997.The Innovator's Dilemma, *Harvard Business School Press*, Boston.

Cooper, R.G. & Kleinschmidt, E.J. 1993.Major new products: What distinguishes the winners in the chemical industry, *Journal of Product Innovation Management* , 2(10), March 1993, pp. 90-111.

Dimitriou, M.2008.(in Greek). *The chemist who won the world of cosmetics.* Accessed [16 March 2012]. Available from the World Wide Web: http://www.isotimia.gr/default.asp?pid=21&la=1&artid=49188&catid=34

Easy Jet.2012. Accessed [15 March 2012]. Available from the World Wide Web:http://www.easyjet.com/EL/Kavie/aboutourfares.html

Govindarajan, V. 2012. *Innovation's Nine Critical Success Factors.* Accessed [27 March 2012]. Available from the World Wide Web: http://blogs.hbr.org/govindarajan/2011/07/innovations-9-critical-success.html

Koutra, P.2009. (in Greek).*G. Korres: Transantlantic the goal of 2010.* Accessed [17 March 2012], Available from the World Wide Web: http://www.euro2day.gr/specials/interviews/133/articles/558803/Article.aspx

Page, A. L.,1993. Assessing New Product Development Practices and Performance: Establishing Crucial Norms, *Journal of Product Innovation Management*, 10(4), pp. 273-290.

Papanikolaou, N. 2010. (in Greek).*Crisis brings airlines together*. Accessed [16 March 2012], Available from the World Wide Web: <
http://www.mensonly.gr/site/content.php?artid=179763>

Pashmore, W. 1994. *Creating Strategic Change*. London:Wiley and Sons.

Rank Xerox, 2012. Company History. Accessed [20 March 2012]. Available from the World Wide Web: < http://www.fundinguniverse.com/company-histories/Xerox-Corporation-Company-History.html>

Smyroglou, F.2010. (in Greek).Cost analysis for setting prices and serving the goals of EASY JET. Accessed [17 March 2012]. Available from:
http://dspace.lib.uom.gr/bitstream/2159/13753/1/Smirloglou_Msc2010.pdf

Stringer,R. 2000.How to manage radical innovation, *California Management Review*, Summer , pp.70-88.

Utterback, J. 1996.Mastering the Dynamics of Innovation, *Harvard Business School Press*.

Waldrop,M. 2001. *The Dream Machine: J.C.R. Licklider and the Revolution That Made Computing Personal*. New York: Viking Penguin.

YOUR KNOWLEDGE HAS VALUE

- We will publish your bachelor's and master's thesis, essays and papers

- Your own eBook and book - sold worldwide in all relevant shops

- Earn money with each sale

Upload your text at www.GRIN.com and publish for free